artbyjanedu

To Finn and Remy
You are our hearts
♥ mama and papa

Hi! I'm Finn.

This is my little brother, Remy.

These are our parents and this is our home.

We love playing ball on the trampoline in our backyard.

"Come on, Papa and Remy, let's go!"

5

"All right, boys, what game do you want to play?" asks Papa.

"Remy, roll the ball to me and then I will roll it to Papa," I say.

Oh no! When Remy rolls the ball, it curves away from me and rolls to Papa.

"What's wrong, Finn?" asks Papa.

"It's not fair!" I say. "Remy was supposed to roll the ball to me, but he rolled it to you instead."

"It's okay, Finn," replies Papa. "Remy tried to roll the ball to you, it just came to me on its own."

"You see, I am a lot bigger than you," explains Papa. "When Remy pushed the ball toward you, it rolled to me because my greater mass warped more of the fabric of the trampoline."

"The ball has to follow the shortest path across the curved surface, which is why it came to me."

I am confused. "Papa, I don't understand that at all."

"Hmm, let me think. How can I explain this?" wonders Papa.

"I've got it!" says Papa with a wink.
"Let's play an imagination game."
He snaps his fingers.

Whoa!!
What is happening?
Is Remy floating?

"Let's imagine that we are astronauts exploring outer space," says Papa.

Imagine that your ball is an asteroid.

"And imagine that the trampoline is flat space."

"Remy pushing the ball is the force that
causes the asteroid to move through space."

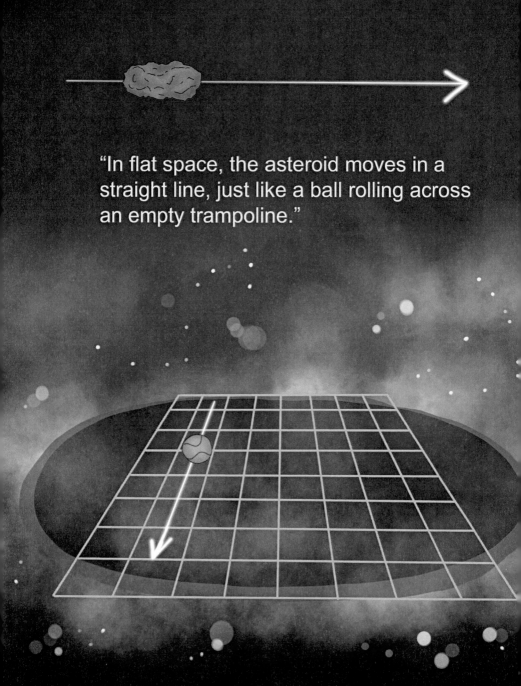

"In flat space, the asteroid moves in a straight line, just like a ball rolling across an empty trampoline."

"When there is an object in space that
has mass—such as the moon—that

So when the asteroid moves close to the moon, the warped space causes the asteroid's path to curve."

"This curvature is what we perceive as gravity."

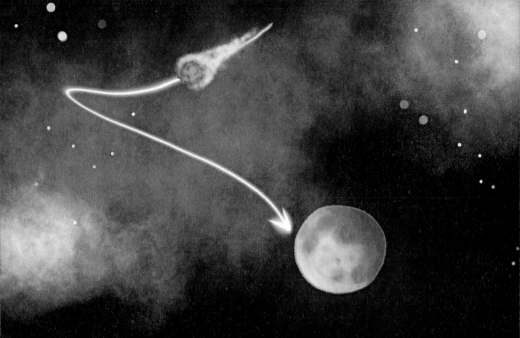

"To us, it *looks like* the asteroid is turning away from its path. . ."

". . . but from the asteroid's frame of reference, it is moving along the shortest path through curved space."

"The most amazing part," says Papa, "is that space contains many more objects than our moon. And every object warps the space around it!"

"The more mass an object has, the more it warps space. And the less mass an object has, the less it warps space."

"So," asks Papa, "between the Earth and the moon, which object do you think has more mass?"

"The Earth has more mass than the moon!" I answer correctly.

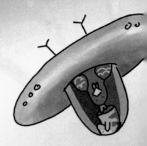

"So if the trampoline represents space, then Papa, you are like the Earth and I am like the moon."

Papa laughs. "That's right!
You've got it!"

"So now," asks Papa, "what do you think happens when Remy pushes the asteroid toward the moon with the Earth nearby?"

"I know!" I shout.

"Because the Earth's mass is greater than the moon's mass, the Earth warps more space than the moon.

So if the asteroid gets too close to the Earth, it will curve toward the Earth instead of the moon."

"Yes!" I shout. "But Papa, I don't want the asteroid to crash into the Earth. We live on Earth!"

"Don't worry," Papa assures me. "Most asteroids are not very big and the friction of Earth's atmosphere causes them to burn up in the sky."

"We call them shooting stars."

"Let's see if we can spot one," says Papa. "Just remember to make a wish when you do!"

Wow! What an adventure. I wonder if Albert Einstein approves of Papa's explanation. What do you think?

Albert Einstein
1879 - 1955

For a lifetime of adventure and imagination,

give wonder
tell stories
create memories

With wonder, our lives are made far richer.

FINN + REMY

Like what you read? Find more books, apparel, and inspirational things on finnandremy.com! We are constantly hard at work creating new books and designs. Available on our website and Amazon.com.

Finn and Remy are originally from Dallas, Texas, but are currently exploring the world with their family. In fact, the concept for this story first developed in Dallas and the book was later written and illustrated in Playa Del Carmen, Mexico, and Medellín, Colombia. Their mom, Jane, loves to draw the boys as little critters and capture their shenanigans (follow her and see the endearing and funny illustrations on FB @finnremy and IG @finnandremy). Dad, Jonathan, does his best to keep those shenanigans in check.